Our Science Fair

by Kama Einhorn
illustrated by David Bergstein

Scott Foresman
is an imprint of

PEARSON

Glenview, Illinois • Boston, Massachusetts • Chandler, Arizona
Upper Saddle River, New Jersey

Illustrations David Bergstein.

Photographs

Every effort has been made to secure permission and provide appropriate credit for photographic material. The publisher deeply regrets any omission and pledges to correct errors called to its attention in subsequent editions.

Unless otherwise acknowledged, all photographs are the property of Pearson Education, Inc.

Photo locators denoted as follows: Top (T), Center (C), Bottom (B), Left (L), Right (R), Background (Bkgd)

8 Peter I. Taylor/PhotoLibrary Group., Inc.

ISBN 13: 978-0-328-50831-0
ISBN 10:   0-328-50831-4

Copyright © by Pearson Education, Inc., or its affiliates. All rights reserved.
Printed in the United States of America. This publication is protected by copyright, and permission should be obtained from the publisher prior to any prohibited reproduction, storage in a retrieval system, or transmission in any form or by any means, electronic, mechanical, photocopying, recording, or likewise. For information regarding permissions, write to Pearson Curriculum Rights & Permissions, One Lake Street, Upper Saddle River, New Jersey 07458.

Pearson® is a trademark, in the U.S. and/or in other countries, of Pearson plc or its affiliates.

Scott Foresman® is a trademark, in the U.S. and/or in other countries, of Pearson Education, Inc., or its affiliates.

7 8 9 10 11 V010 17 16 15 14 13

"We're having a science fair," Miss Heath said. "Each grade will enter a project. We'll work together. People from the village will come to watch us at the fair."

3

"What can we do?" Miss Heath asked.

"Let's make a new kind of shoe!" said Joe.

"Let's study apes!" cried Lana.

"We're studying volcanoes," said Billy. "Let's build a volcano model."
"Yes! We can show how a volcano erupts," the others agreed.

We got an empty soda bottle. We molded dough around it. We tried to make it pretty. We filled the bottle with warm water and red food coloring. We added soap and baking soda.

At the fair, we added vinegar to our volcano. It erupted perfectly. The red foam looked like hot lava flowing down the sides.

Guess who won first place? We did!

Everyday Experiments

Scientists around the world study and work together on different kinds of experiments. Studying volcanoes helps us understand how they form and erupt. It can also help us identify the warning signs of an eruption. Knowing the warning signs can help us save the lives of people who live near volcanoes. All scientists experiment, test their ideas, and draw conclusions from their studies.

Scientists install a GPS receiver on a volcano. The receiver can give eruption warning signs.